Revise and Test

CW00621579

Bookkeeping and Accounts 1

Geoffrey Whitehead BSc(Econ)

Series Adviser: Geoffrey Whitehead BSc(Econ)

Pitman

Using this 'Revise and Test' booklet

1   The 'Revise and Test' series is in question and answer form. It will help you revise everything you need to know about your particular syllabus. The questions are detailed and rigorous, and cannot be answered always with one word. It follows that the first time you go over a topic you may be learning the material rather than testing yourself. It is not just a self-testing book, but a self-teaching book too!

2   The first time you study a topic you may need to go over it two or three times. Then put a tick against the topic number on the check list at the back of the book.

3   Subsequently you should revise the topic at intervals, especially just before a monthly test or an examination. Each time you revise it put in a further tick.

4   If you find a topic particularly difficult put a ring round the number. This will remind you to do it again soon. Practice makes perfect.

5   Finally remember that learning facts is relatively easy. Applying them in written work is more difficult. Each topic has one piece of written work and you should find others from textbooks and past examination papers. Remember the saying 'Writing maketh an exact man'. Don't worry about who is going to mark your written work. You can appraise it for yourself! Keep writing!

1 Basic ideas on bookkeeping

1 What is bookkeeping?

It is the keeping of routine financial records in books of account.

2 What are the chief books of account?

The ledger, the cash book and the daybooks (or journals).

3 Which of these is the chief book of account?

The ledger. It gets its name because in the medieval counting houses it lay open ready for use on a ledge under the window, where the bookkeeper had a good light.

4 What do we call the pages of the ledger?

Accounts.

5 What do they keep account of?

They keep account of the business's transactions with the person or thing named at the top of the page.

6 What does the cash book keep account of?

The cheques and cash received and paid.

7 Why do we need bookkeeping records?

(a) To keep track of the money we owe people, and the money people owe us. (b) To enable us to calculate what profit we are making.

8 What are the consequences of failing to make profits?

We are forced out of business, either for fear of losing all the money we had when we started or because we are unable to pay our debts and are made bankrupt.

9 What is accountancy?

It is a profession whose members practise accounting (the keeping of accounts).

10 What is an accountant?

A member of the accountancy profession.

11 How does bookkeeping differ from accounting?

Only in degree. Bookkeeping is the keeping of routine accounting records. Accounting is the presentation, analysis and interpreting of routine accounts to control and manage a business enterprise.

Go over the topic again until you are sure of all the answers. Then tick it off on the check list at the back of the book.

2 The ledger

1 What is the ledger?

It is the main book of account.

2 Does it have to be a bound book?

No. It can be a loose leaf book, with the accounts arranged in alphabetical order, or it can be a part of some computer memory, which the computer can access as and when required.

3 What do we enter in the ledger?

Every transaction that takes place, whether it is the purchase or sale of goods, the supply of services or the payment of money in cash or cheques.

4 How many entries does each transaction require?

Two. That is why bookkeeping is called 'double-entry' bookkeeping.

5 Why does each transaction require two entries?

Because for every transaction there must be two accounts affected. If A pays money to B, A is the giver and loses money, while B is the receiver and gains money. We must therefore make an entry in both accounts.

6 What are the pages in the ledger called?

Accounts – each double page (i.e. both sides of the same page) is called 'an account'.

7 What appears at the top of the page?

The name of the person, or thing being recorded. Thus we can have accounts for Tom Jones, Penelope Whitehead, etc., or accounts for things (such as furniture and fittings) or of expenses (such as postage or telephone expenses).

8 What are the three classes of accounts?

Personal accounts, nominal accounts and real accounts.

9 What is a personal account?

It is a page in the ledger which is headed with the name and address of a person with whom the business deals. It keeps a record of our transactions with that person.

10 What are the two big classes of persons we deal with?

The debtors (who owe us money) and the creditors (to whom we owe money)

11 Which are more numerous, the debtors or the creditors?

Usually the debtors, because we sell to a great many customers but we buy our raw materials from a very few suppliers.

However – a few firms might have very few customers and quite a large number of suppliers. Creditors would then be more numerous.

12 Give an example of a firm with very few customers

Armament manufacturers. They usually only sell to friendly governments.

13 Explain this ruling of paper

Dr										Cr
										L127
Date		Details	F	£	p	Date		Details	F	£	p

Fig. 2.1 Ruled ledger paper

(a) It is ledger paper. (b) The thick line divides the page into two halves. (c) The two sides are called the debit side and the credit side of the account. (d) Both sides are ruled up with columns for the date, details, folio numbers and the amount.

14 What are the rules for making entries on ledger paper?

(a) Debit the account that receives goods or services or money. (b) Credit the account that gives goods or services or money.

15 We have sold Tom Brown on credit, goods worth £250. What entries shall we make?

Debit Tom Brown's account with £250. He has received goods. Credit the sales account with £250. The sales account is one of the accounts of our business and we have given him goods worth £250.

16 Explain these three accounts

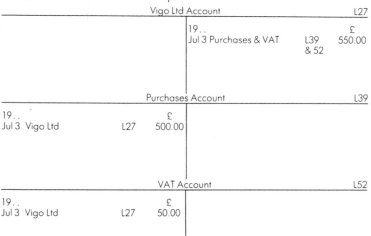

Vigo Ltd Account					L27
		19. .			£
		Jul 3 Purchases & VAT	L39 & 52		550.00

Purchases Account				L39
19. .		£		
Jul 3 Vigo Ltd	L27	500.00		

VAT Account				L52
19. .		£		
Jul 3 Vigo Ltd	L27	50.00		

Fig. 2.2

(a) Vigo Ltd gave us goods to the value of £550.00 (including VAT at 10 per cent). They are creditors as a result (we owe them the money). (b) The goods have been received by us, so we debit our Purchases account with £500. (c) The VAT is VAT input tax on purchases we have made, so we can reclaim it from the VAT inspector. We therefore debit it in VAT account as he is a debtor for this amount. (d) The folio numbers are cross-references, to show us where the other half of the double entry can be found.

17 What are real accounts?

Accounts which keep a record of assets, real things that we own. They may be called typewriter account, plant and machinery account, etc.

18 What is the rule for making entries on real accounts?

Debit the asset account when we purchase the asset. Credit the asset account if we depreciate the asset or sell it off at the end of its useful life.

19 What is a nominal account?

An account where the money is there in name only (as a matter of record). This occurs with all losses, i.e. expenses (rent, light and heat etc.). The money has actually been spent on these items. It also applies to all profits. The actual money has been received and put into the cash account or the bank account, but a record of it is kept in the nominal account, for example, 'commission received account'.

20 What is the rule for making entries in these accounts?

Debit the losses (e.g. debit rent paid account). Credit the profits (e.g. credit rent received from tenants account).

Written Exercise: *Make the entries for the following transactions in the appropriate ledger accounts. (a) M Smith supplies us with goods valued at £600 + VAT £60 on 17 January 19. . (b) On 31 January the account is paid in full £660 by cheque.*

Go over the topic again until you are sure of all the answers. Then tick it off on the check list at the back of the book.

3 Business Documents

1 What is the importance of business documents?

They are the starting point for every business activity. No one wants to do anything until they have a document which triggers the action and creates a legal obligation on both parties interested in the transaction.

2 List the common business documents

(a) Invoices. (b) Credit notes. (c) Debit notes. (d) Statements.

3 What is an invoice?

A document made out by the seller whenever one person sends goods to another.

4 What details does it contain?

(a) The names and addresses of both parties to the transaction. (b) Details of the goods or services to be supplied. (c) If it is for goods it gives the unit price, the quantity and the total value. (d) The trade discount (if any). (e) The VAT charged (and the seller's VAT number). (f) The date of the transaction. (g) The terms of sale, i.e. cash discount (if any) and time of payment.

5 What will the unit price be on the invoice?

It can be the recommended retail price to the consumer, in which case trade discount will be given to enable the retailer to make a profit. It can be the trade price as shown in the supplier's trade catalogue or trade price list.

6 If VAT is 15 per cent what is the VAT on an order valued at £385?

10 per cent =	£38.50
5 per cent =	£19.25 (half the above)
Total VAT =	£57.75

7 How would you check an invoice before passing it for payment?

(a) Are the goods as ordered? (b) Are the prices correct? (c) Are the discounts correct? (d) Have the calculations been done correctly? (e) Have the goods actually arrived and been taken into stores in good order and condition?

8 How many copies does an invoice have?

Usually at least four: (a) a top copy for the customer's accounts department; (b) a second copy for our accounts department; (c) a delivery note for our delivery van – the driver gets it signed when the goods are delivered; (d) an advice note packed with the goods in our dispatch department. There may also be (e) a representative's copy.

9 What is a credit note?

A document (usually printed in red) which is made out by a seller to whom goods have been returned.

10 What details does it have on it?

The same details as an invoice, e.g. addresses, details of the goods, etc. but the entries in the account will be the reverse of those with an invoice as we have to reduce the customer's debt because some of the goods have effectively been returned.

11 When is a credit note made out, apart from when goods are returned?

(a) When an overcharge has been made on an invoice. (b) When an allowance is made on goods because they are not up to standard.

12 What is a debit note?

The opposite of a credit note (and therefore similar to an invoice). It is made out: (a) to correct an invoice where there has been an undercharge; (b) to charge a customer with some extra charge, such as carriage, insurance, interest on an overdue account, etc. It may also be used by a customer returning goods – and will then trigger the supplier into making out a credit note.

13 What is a statement of account?	A statement sent out each month to customers requesting payment for goods or services supplied in the month.
14 When is it sent out?	Usually on the last day of the month, but some firms use 'cyclical billing' – send out 4 per cent of all statements each working day. This avoids over-activity at the end of the month.
15 How would you check a statement?	(a) Compare it with the ledger account. (b) Make allowances for goods in transit (either in or out – as returns) and for payments in transit by post or credit transfers.

Written Exercise: *Here is a set of invoices. Write a full explanation of all the items on the document, and the use of the extra copies behind.*

Go over the topic again until you are sure of all the answers. Then tick it off on the check list at the back of the book.

4 Journals and daybooks

1 What is the meaning of 'journal'?	It is just the French word for 'daybook'.
2 What is the importance of daybooks?	They are the books of original entry, which make permanent records of the documents coming into, and going out of, a business.
3 What was the original daybook?	The journal proper, usually just called the journal. Every document was recorded in the journal proper, to give a double entry – debiting one account and crediting another.

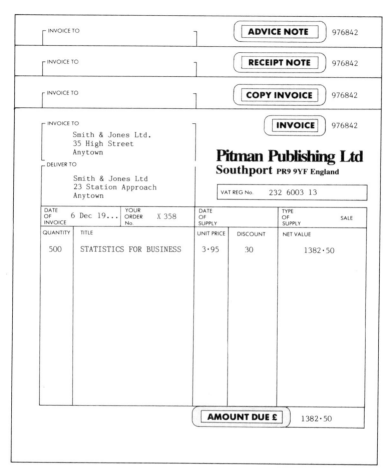

INVOICE TO				**ADVICE NOTE**		976842

INVOICE TO				**RECEIPT NOTE**		976842

INVOICE TO				**COPY INVOICE**		976842

INVOICE TO

Smith & Jones Ltd.
35 High Street
Anytown

DELIVER TO

Smith & Jones Ltd
23 Station Approach
Anytown

INVOICE 976842

Pitman Publishing Ltd
Southport PR9 9YF England

VAT REG No.   232 6003 13

DATE OF INVOICE	6 Dec 19...	YOUR ORDER No.	X 358	DATE OF SUPPLY		TYPE OF SUPPLY	SALE
QUANTITY	TITLE			UNIT PRICE	DISCOUNT	NET VALUE	
500	STATISTICS FOR BUSINESS			3·95	30	1382·50	

AMOUNT DUE £   1382·50

Fig. 3.1 A four-copy invoice set

4 What happened to this original journal?

Those entries that occurred repeatedly, like sales invoices, purchases invoices, and credit notes in and out were removed from it and put in specialist daybooks. This left the journal with just the rarer items – items which don't occur every day.

5 List these rarer entries that now appear in the journal as journal entries

(a) Opening journal entries when a business starts. (b) The purchase of assets. (c) The sale of assets. (d) Depreciation entries. (e) Bad debts. (f) The correction of errors. (g) Closing journal entries, made on the last day of the financial year.

6 What are the other daybooks called?

(a) The purchases daybook. (b) The sales daybook. (c) The purchases returns book. (d) The sales returns book.

7 What is an opening journal entry?

An entry made out on the first day a business starts up. It lists the assets brought in by the proprietor(s), and the external liabilities already incurred (if any). It also calculates the capital due to the proprietor(s).

8 What is capital?

It is what the business owes back to the owner of the business. It is not money, as most people think. The proprietor may bring in money, but he/she may also bring in machinery, tools, furniture, premises, etc. The total value of all these things is the capital contributed by the proprietor.

9 Explain this journal entry

19.. Jan 1			Dr (£)	Cr (£)
	Premises	L1	27 000.00	
	Machinery	L2	8 590.00	
	Loose Tools	L3	1 450.00	
	Motor Van	L4	1 680.00	
	Bank	CB1	2 324.75	
	Cash	CB1	196.25	
	A. Nichols	L5		13 747.00
	B. Nichols	L6		27 494.00
	Being assets and liabilities at this date		£41 241.00	41 241.00

(a) It is an opening journal entry for a partnership business. (b) It lists all the assets in the debit column. (c) There are no external liabilities. (d) The two liabilities are to the partners for capital contributed. (e) They seem to be sharing the business in the proportions of two thirds to one third with B. Nichols having the larger share.

Written Exercise: *Write an opening journal entry for R. Miller's business which starts on 5 May 19.. with assets as follows: premises £22 500, greenhouses £16 000, equipment £5148, bank account £500, cash £78.50. There is one external liability, agricultural bank loan account £35 000.*

Go over the topic again until you are sure of all the answers. Then tick it off on the check list at the back of the book.

5 Entries in the daybooks

1 Figure 5.1 (see page 12) shows a purchases daybook. Explain the entries

(a) The three invoices from the three suppliers have been entered to give a permanent record. (b) Two of them gave trade discount at 40 per cent. (c) VAT was charged on the net price to R. Wilks. (d) The three invoices and two of the totals have been posted to the relevant accounts.

2 Explain what you would have done in posting these entries to the accounts

(a) The three invoice totals £16.94, £33.42 and £26.87 would be credited to the suppliers' accounts in the ledger. The suppliers are all creditors who have given the goods – we credit the giver of goods. (b) The total purchases figure is £70.21. This has to be debited to the purchases account. We have received these goods, so we debit the receiver. The purchases account must be page 63 in the ledger. (c) VAT is £7.02. We shall have to pay this to the suppliers as it is included in the invoices. This £7.02 is debited to VAT account and will reduce the VAT payable to Customs and Excise.

Date	Day	Details	Fol.	£	£	VAT (10%) £	£
19.. Jan	4	R. Mitchell 4 kgs fluorescent powder @ £3.85 kg	L27		15.40	1.54	16.94
	15	M. Lancer 12 metres non-flam. cloth @ £4.22 m Less trade discount 40%		50.64 20.26	30.38	3.04	33.42
	29	M. Rossendale 4 litres fluorescent paint @ £3.85 litre 3 metres 'safety-first' wallboard @ £8.44 metre Less trade discount 40%	L33	15.40 25.32 40.72 16.29			
			L41		24.43	2.44	26.87
				£	70.21	7.02	77.23
					L63	L62	

Fig. 5.1 Purchases daybook in R. Wilks' business

3 Is this going to give a perfect double entry?

Yes, £77.23 on the debit side (in purchases account and VAT account). £77.23 on the credit side in the three supplier's accounts.

4 Is trade discount ever posted to an account?

No. It never enter the accounts at all.

5 Suppose this illustration had been of the Sales daybook what invoices would we be entering in this book?

The second copies of our own invoices. (The top copies would have been sent to our customers.

6 Would there be any differences in the records?

No – but the postings to the ledger would have been different. The personal accounts of the customers would be debited (they are receiving the goods we sold to them). The total sales would be credited in the sales account (credit the giver since we have given the goods). The VAT account will be credited with the total VAT. It is our output tax, and we owe it to the VAT inspector, who is a creditor for the amount.

7 Here is this week's bunch of one kind of credit note. Are they for purchases returned, or sales returned?

Purchases returns – they are all different shapes and sizes. If they were sales returns we would have made them out ourselves on our own credit notes and they would all be the same shape and size.

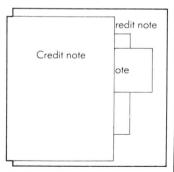

Fig. 5.2 Credit notes

8 How can you tell a credit note from an invoice?	They're usually printed in red.
9 What is an analytical sales day book?	A sales daybook that has extra analysis columns to enable us to analyse sales in various ways.
10 What ways, for example?	We might analyse them under sales areas to check up on representatives and determine their activity and commission. We might analyse them A–E, F–M, N–S, T–Z to help prepare control accounts for the sales ledger. We might analyse them under products to determine sales activity in each product area – it might change our production plans

Written Exercise: *Imagine you have returned the three metres of wallboard to M Rossendale mentioned in Fig. 5.1. What document will Rossendale send you; which book will it be entered in; how will the double entry be done, and what will the debits and credits be?*

Go over the topic again until you are sure of all the answers. Then tick it off on the check list at the back of the book.

6 More journal entries

1 What kinds of entries go in the journal proper besides opening journal entries?	All unusual items (i.e. not purchases or sales items, or returns). The common ones are: (a) purchases of capital items (assets); (b) depreciation of assets; (c) sales of assets; (d) writing off of bad debts; (e) corrections of errors.
2 What sort of entry is this?	It is the purchase of an asset (furniture) for £1840 from A Dealer Ltd.

19..						
Jan	4	Furniture and Fittings A/c	Dr	L5	1840.00	
		A. Dealer Ltd A/c		L71		1840.00

Fig. 6.1

3 How do you know it is a purchase and not a sale?

Because the asset account is debited. The rule for purchase of an asset is 'always debit the asset account and credit the firm that gave you the goods'.

4 Supposing you paid in cash or by cheque for this furniture?

Then instead of crediting the supplier we would credit either cash account or bank account. Since we credited A Dealer Ltd we haven't paid yet for the goods.

5 What does every journal entry end in?

A narration – a sentence explaining what has been done. It usually starts with the word 'Being' and ends with 'at this date'.

6 Write a suitable narration for the journal entry in Fig. 6.1

Being purchase of desks, chairs and book-cases for the personnel department at this date.

7 What sort of a journal entry is shown in Fig. 6.2?

It is a depreciation entry. Ten per cent of the value of the furniture in Fig. 6.1 has been written off at the end of the year.

19..
Dec
	31	Depreciation A/c
		    Furniture etc. A/c
		Being depreciation for one
		    year on Personnel Dept.
		    furniture, at this date.
			Dr	L16
				L5
					184.00	184.00

Fig. 6.2

8 What sort of an account is depreciation account?

It is one of the nominal accounts in the nominal ledger (sometimes called the general ledger).

9 What does 'nominal' mean?

It means 'in name only'. We are keeping a record of money in name only. The money itself has either been lost – in this case by fair wear and tear – or it could have been gained if the account was a profit account – such as rent received or commission received.

10 What happens to all the nominal accounts at the end of the financial year?

They are cleared into the final accounts (the trading account and the profit and loss account) to enable us to work out the profit or loss for the whole year.

11 What sort of journal entry is this?

It is also a depreciation entry but instead of the depreciation being written off the asset account it is collected together in a 'provision for depreciation on plant account'.

| 19.. Dec | 31 | Depreciation A/c   Dr
   Provision for Depreciation A/c
Being depreciation on Plant and
   Machinery at this date. | L16
L17 | 2350.00 | 2350.00 |

Fig. 6.3

12 What is the idea of that?

It helps us comply with the Companies Acts 1948–81, which require us to show the assets on the balance sheet at their original cost, less the depreciation to date. The asset stays on the books at cost price, but the depreciation is collected together in a separate provision account.

13 How will this appear on the balance sheet?

As follows:

	Less	
Plant and machinery	Deprecia-tion	Value
£	£	£
58 725.50	(23 250.00)	35 475.50

14 What happens when we sell a worn-out asset at the end of its working life?

It will have a certain value on our books. When we sell it we may sell it for (a) exactly that value (b) more than the value (a profit on sale) or (c) less than the value (a loss on sale).

15 What is the vital rule for making the journal entry on sales of assets?

We must **remove the book value** from the books. Any difference is either a profit or a loss and goes to sale of . . .

account (e.g. sale of motor vehicles account).

16 I sell a typewriter valued at £80 on the books for £30 cash. What will the journal entry be?

To remove the book value we have to credit typewriters account with £80. We only have £30 to debit in cash account. The balance is £50 debited (a loss) in sale of typewriters account.

| 19..
Mar | 17 | Cash A/c
Sale of typewriters A/c
   Typewriters A/c
Being sale of typewriter
  at this date | Dr
Dr | 30.00
50.00 | 80.00 |

17 What sort of journal entry is shown in Fig. 6.4?

It is a bad debts entry. A debtor owes us £100 but is only able to pay £30. The rest has to be written off to Bad Debts account.

| 19..
Sep | 19 | Bad Debts A/c
Bank A/c
   A. Debtor | Dr
Dr | 70.00
30.00 | 100.00 |

Fig. 6.4

18 What sort of an account is bad debts account?

A nominal account, one of the losses of the business. The loss will be written off the profits at the end of the year.

19 Why is it difficult to learn how to do corrections of errors?

Because every error is different – there can be hundreds of different types of errors. The rule is 'Find out what is wrong – and make the necessary entries to put it right'.

20 What does 'the necessary entries' mean?

It means that some accounts may need to be debited and some may need to be credited. You debit and credit accounts as necessary to correct the

17

error. (The correction of errors is dealt with specially in Topic 13).

Written Exercise: *Write journal entries for each of the following events. (a) On 1 January 19. . A Smith buys an electric forge for £865. (b) On 31 December he depreciates it by 20 per cent. (c) On the same day he sells it for £600 as he finds it inconvenient to use except for a few minor jobs.*

Go over the topic again until you are sure of all the answers. Then tick it off on the check list at the back of the book.

7 The three-column cash book

1 What is the three-column cash book?

The main type of cash book used in large businesses to record the movements of both cash and cheques. See Fig. 7.1 opposite.

2 What is special about it?

It is both a book of original entry and a ledger account – in fact two ledger accounts.

3 What accounts are these?

The cash account and the bank account, which appear side by side on the page.

4 Why are these accounts separated from the main ledger?

For security reasons. We cannot have everyone tampering with the cash account and the bank account.

5 Who keeps this book then?

The chief cashier – usually an experienced and trusted member of staff.

6 What is the third column for on each side of the book?

The discount column, discount allowed on the debit side and discount received on the credit side.

7 Are these discount columns also a ledger account?

No, they are only memorandum columns, to remind us about the discount.

Debit (Dr)

19..	Details	F	Discount £	Cash £	Bank £
Jan 1	Balance	b/d		325.50	1 726.50
1	Sales	L3		825.60	48.00
2	M. Smith	L21	2.53		
2	T. Brown	L27		7.56	
3	Sales	L3		1 370.60	2 000.00
3	Cash	C		2 428.50	
4	Sales	L3			
4	M. Yardley	L44	4.51	2 569.60	85.60
5	Cash	C			4 000.00
5	Sales	L3		3 128.50	
		£	7.04	10 655.86	7 860.10
			£ 1.82		
19.. Jan 8	Balance	b/d		£ 4 633.12	£ 7 531.57

Credit (Cr)

19..	Details	F	Discount £	Cash £	Bank £
Jan 1	Stationery	L19			15.49
2	Fares	L17		7.24	
2	Postage	L61			186.50
2	Petty cash	PcB5			50.00
3	Bank	C		2 000.00	
4	Cleaning expenses	L40	1.96		76.54
4	Repairs	L52		15.50	
5	Bank	C		4 000.00	
5	Balance	c/d		4 633.12	7 531.57
		£	1.96	10 655.86	7 860.10
			£ 1.81		

Fig. 7.1 A three-column cash book

8 What type of accounts are the cash and bank accounts?

Real accounts, recording assets, cash in hand and cash at bank.

9 What is the rule for making entries in these accounts?

Debit the account if it receives money (or a cheque). Credit the account if it gives money (or a cheque).

10 What is a contra entry in the cash book?

The word 'contra' means 'opposite' (to contradict is to say the opposite). With a contra entry both sides of the entry can be seen on the page of the cash book on opposite sides. Remember that the cash book is the only book where two accounts appear on the same page. So we see one half in the cash account and the other half in the bank account.

11 What tells us the entry is a contra entry?

We write a C in the folio column on each side of the book.

12 Can a contra entry appear like this anywhere else in the ledger?

No – because this is the only place where we have two accounts side by side.

13 How do we post the cash book to the ledger?

(a) All items on the debit side of the cash book are credited in the accounts to which they are posted (except the total of the discount allowed column). (b) All items on the credit side of the cash book are debited to the accounts to which they are posted (except the total of the discount received account). (c) The totals of the discount columns are the only things that don't change sides.

14 Why is the total discount allowed debited to discount allowed account?

Because it is one of the losses of the business – and all losses become debits.

15 Why is the total discount received credited in discount received account?

Because it is one of the profits of the business and all profits become credits on their accounts.

Written Exercise: *Enter the following items on 5 May 19. . in a three-column* *cash book. Balance in hand, cash £27.50, bank £1078.25. Received cheque from R Lancelot £19 in full settlement of a debt of £20. Paid telephone expenses by cheque £308.50. Paid for postage stamps in cash £12.50. Paid rent £125.00 by cheque. Cash sales £1048.50. Banked £850. Balance the book at the end of the day and bring down the balance.*

Go over the topic again until you are sure of all the answers. Then tick it off on the check list at the back of the book.

8 The VAT account

1 What sort of account is the VAT account?

It is the personal account of H.M. Customs and Excise Department.

2 Is the Department a debtor or a creditor?

It can be either. If we trade in standard rated goods, and therefore collect a lot of tax from our customers, we shall owe this tax to the Department and it will be a creditor.

3 When will it be a debtor?

If we are a trader in zero-rated goods (chiefly food) we shall not collect tax from our customers, but we shall pay tax on many of our expenses and shall be entitled to a refund of this tax. So the Department will be a debtor.

4 What do we call the tax we collect on our supplies to customers?

Output tax.

5 What do we call tax we pay on the things we buy from our suppliers?

Input tax.

6 How much VAT is payable to H.M. Customs?

Tax payable = Output tax − Input tax.

7 Here is a typical VAT account. Explain it

The input tax is on the debit side. The output tax is on the credit side. As the output tax exceeds the input tax the balance of £3026 is payable to Customs and Excise Department.

VAT Account   L92

19..		£	19..		£
Jun 30	Sundry purchases	1 427.50	Jun 30	Sundry sales	4 285.25
30	Cash purchases	14.25	30	Cash sales	182.50
30	Balance	3 026.00			
		£4 467.75			£4 467.75
			19..		£
			Jul 1	Balance	3 026.00

Fig. 8.1 A VAT account

8 Where would the balance on the VAT account appear on the balance sheet at the end of the year?

Either as a current asset (part of the debtors) if H.M. Customs owe us a refund, or as a current liability (part of the creditors) if we owe output tax to H.M. Customs.

Written Exercise: *Tom Smith is a grocer, selling zero rated items only. In March he buys equipment, petrol etc., with tax of £37.95. Show the VAT account for March. At March 1 Customs and Excise owed him £83 which they paid by cheque on 15 March. Balance off the account on 31 March and bring the balance down. Who owes whom how much?*

Go over the topic again until you are sure of all the answers. Then tick it off on the check list at the back of the book.

9 The petty cash book

1 What is the petty cash book?

A specially ruled book which enables a young person to take care of small items of cash, using a system called the imprest system.

2 How does the imprest system work?

The chief cashier decides how much cash is required for one week to run the simple day-to-day expenses of the office (e.g. postage, messenger's fares and minor payments of all sorts). Suppose this is £50 per week. It becomes the 'imprest', the sum of money given to the petty cashier, and recorded in the petty cash book. At the end of the week, once all payments have been recorded, the cashier checks the book and restores the imprest to its original £50 ready for the next week.

3 How is the petty cash book ruled?

As shown in Fig. 9.1 overleaf.

4 Explain the ruling

(a) The 'centre' of the page is offset towards the left-hand side. (b) The debit side is reduced to a single money column, and the details about the debit entries are written in the details column on the credit side. (c) The credit side is extended to include several analysis columns. Only the first column headed 'Total' is the real credit side of the account, in which all money paid out (credit the giver) is entered. Each amount is then analysed off into columns where the various expenses can be collected together, postage, travelling expenses, etc. The last column, 'Ledger A/Cs', is different from the rest, and has a separate column for folio numbers alongside it.

5 What did the petty cashier do on 4 April?

Drew the imprest of £100 and paid postage £27.30.

6 What happened on 8 April?

The petty cashier collected cash from members of staff for private telephone calls – and also gave the dustman a tip for clearing rubbish.

7 On balancing the book on 9 April what should we find about the various totals in the analysis columns?

They should cross-tot to come to the same result as the Total column.

Debit Side / Credit Side PCB 17

£	p	Date	Details	PCV	Total £	Total p	Postage £	Postage p	Travelling £	Travelling p	Stationery £	Stationery p	Sundry Expenses £	Sundry Expenses p	Ledger A/Cs £	Ledger A/Cs p
100	=	19.. Apr.4	Imprest received	CB/74												
		4	Postage stamps	1	27	30	27	30								
		5	Train fares (Reading)	2	9	65			9	65						
		5	Envelopes	3	13	65					13	65				
		6	Recorded delivery letters	4	4	25	4	25								
		6	Cleaning materials	5	3	65							3	65		
		6	Bus fares	6	11	68			11	68						
		7	Refreshments for visitors	7	8	26							8	26		
		7	T. Smith	8	11	24									11	24
18	42	8	Telephone cash received	£42												
		8	Gratuity (rubbish clearance)	9	1	11							1	11		
		9	Postage stamps	10	14	25	14	25								
					93	93	45	80	10	33	13	65	12	91	11	24
		9	Balance	c/d	24	49	(£25)		(£33)		(£13)		(£73)		L17	
£118	42				£118	42									11	24
24	49	11	Balance	b/d												
75	51	11	Imprest restored by cashier	CB/87												

Fig. 9.1 The ruling of a petty cash book

8 What happens to the total of the Postage column?	It is debited in the postage account as one of the losses (expenses) of the business.
9 What happens to the £11.24 paid to T Smith?	It is debited in T Smith's account. He was a creditor, but we have now paid him the money in cash to clear the account. Debit Smith, as he has received money.
10 What happens to the £18.42 telephone money collected?	The money itself is in the petty cashier's till and will offset some of the expenditure. The £18.42 is posted to the credit side of the telephone account (L42). It reduces the expenditure for telephones when we come to do the final accounts at the end of the year.
11 Why does the cashier only need to restore the £75.51 at the end of the week, when the petty cashier spent £93.93?	Because the difference (£18.42) was collected from the staff for telephone calls.
12 What are the advantages of the imprest system?	(a) It saves the chief cashier being bothered for trifling sums of money. (b) It is good training for a young person, with a simple method of bookkeeping. (c) The small sum involved is not much of a temptation to either another member of staff or to the petty cashier. (d) The analysis columns collect many small items together and reduce posting to the ledger – they can all be done in one entry.

Written Exercise: *Rule up a petty cash book the same as Fig. 9.1 and make the following entries. Balance the account at the end of the week.*

Mar 1 Balance b/d £45.50 and imprest of £54.50 restored (to bring to £100).

Mar 2 Stationery expenses £4.25; paid for coffee, tea, etc., £2.10.

Mar 3 Paid for stamps £11.60; staff fares £8.60.

Mar 4 Paid traveller's hotel expenses £15.50; collected £4.75 from a staff member for an international call (telephone a/c).

Mar 5 Paid for stationery £12.30; postage £4.50.

Go over the topic again until you are sure of all the answers. Then tick it off on the check list at the back of the book.

10 Other ways of keeping original entries

1 What is the main problem with daybooks?

They make an awful lot of work, and most of it is just copying information from invoices, credit notes, etc. to give a permanent record.

2 How can we get over this difficulty?

We have to devise some simple method of preserving the detailed information in the documents, so that we have a permanent record of them. We must of course make the entries in the ledger accounts, debiting and crediting as necessary.

3 How can we arrange this?

There are three ways: (a) the slip system; (b) a three-in-one system (or simultaneous records system); (c) a computerised system.

4 What is the slip system?

Any system where the bookkeeping entries are made direct from the document – the slip – into the ledger accounts concerned. Suppose we send out 20 invoices in a day. The second copies will come down to the accounts department to be entered. Instead of entering them in a sales daybook we **batch them up** – add up the values on a printing calculator and get the total of the 20 invoices. Clip the slip of paper from the calculator on to the top copy. If VAT is involved do the same for the VAT on all the invoices. Now: (a) post the sales invoices to the separate accounts of all the debtors (debit each debtor); (b) credit sales account with the total sales figure and VAT account with the output tax charged to the customers; (c) file the invoices away in a binder so they can be turned up if we want to know the details of what was sold.

5 That seems simple enough for sales invoices. What is the difficulty about doing the same thing for purchases invoices?

The trouble is they are all different shapes and sizes. Not quite such neat things to file away. We may need to use lever arch files instead of invoice binders. It is easy enough really.

6 When it comes to credit notes are there any problems?

No – the sales returns credit notes are sent out by us and are all the same size and shape. The purchases returns credit notes will again be all different shapes and sizes.

7 What are the advantages of this system?

(a) You save a lot of time. (b) The cost of daybooks is avoided. (The disadvantage is that you do not have a permanent record of the sales and purchases, just a bound or filed collection of invoices).

8 What is a 3 in 1 system?

Any system where more than one record is made simultaneously. The correct accounting name is therefore 'simultaneous records' systems.

9 How does a simultaneous records system work?

The supplier of the system (a firm such as Kalamazoo Ltd – a famous name for these systems) supplies specially ruled papers. These are placed one on top of the other, with carbon paper in between. Suppose we have (a) a sales daybook sheet with; (b) a ledger card on top of it; and (c) a statement on top of that.

When we enter the sale on the statement it will appear on the ledger card and the daybook below. When we enter the next invoice we take the statement and ledger card for the firm concerned, position it over the next clean line on the daybook sheet and make the entry. This writes up the statement, the ledger and the daybook simultaneously.

10 What are the effects of this system?

(a) The statement is always ready to be sent out to the customer. (b) The customer's ledger account is always up to date. (c) The daybook is always complete, except that we don't write out the full details. (d) We file the invoices and they are available if we need the full details. (e) The sales account and VAT account can be updated by posting the total columns on the daybook sheet.

11 How does a computerised system work?

Very similarly, except that we let the computer do all the work. The procedure is: (a) batch up the documents as before to give a lot of similar entries; (b) turn them into machine entries either by using punched cards or a key-edit device; (c) the computer now accepts these entries and the programs do the following things: (i) check the validity of all the inputs and print out a list of entries and a list of items rejected; (ii) debit or credit all the relevant accounts to do a proper double entry; (iii) update the accounts ready to do a trial balance whenever we request it; (iv) let us view any account on a visual display unit if we wish to; (v) print out a copy of any account if we want a hard copy; (vi) print out a complete audit trail if we want to see where every entry went.

Written Exercise: *Explain what is meant by a 'simultaneous records' system. Imagine you have to keep a sales ledger with this system – that is a sales daybook, the ledger accounts and the statement. Explain what you would need to do.*

Go over the topic again until you are sure of all the answers. Then tick it off on the check list at the back of the book.

11 The trial balance

1 What is a trial balance?

It is a list of balances extracted from the ledger accounts to discover whether the bookkeeping has been done correctly.

2 How often do we take out a trial balance?

Usually once a month, but we can do it more frequently if we like.

3 What should happen when we list the balances on the accounts?

Those with debit balances are listed in the debit (left-hand) column and those with credit balances in the credit (right-hand) column. If we have made perfect double entries, the two columns should add up to the same figure, i.e. the trial balance should balance.

4 What types of accounts will we have in the debit column?

(a) The purchases account. (b) The sales returns account. (c) All the assets, opening stock, land and building, plant and machinery, debtors, etc. (d) All the losses (expenses) of the business, light and heat, telephones, etc. (e) The drawings accounts.

5 What types of accounts will we have in the credit column?

(a) The sales account. (b) The purchases returns account. (c) All the liabilities, loans, bank overdraft (if any), creditors, etc. (d) Any profits – such as rent received or commission received. (e) The capital account.

6 Supposing the trial balance doesn't balance?

There must be an error somewhere in the hundreds of entries made during the month.

7 How should we set about finding it?

There is a detailed list of things to do to investigate the problem, but first we should check that everything is on the correct side. So go through every item and see if it obeys the rules in (4) and (5) above. (Rent paid account is a loss – so it should be on the debit side – etc., etc.).

8 What is the list of things we do to eliminate the error?

(a) Add up the columns again to make sure we haven't made a slip. (b) Check the extractions from the ledger – have we made a slip in listing the balances? (c) Is the error just 1 out, in any column, i.e. 1000, 100, 10, 0.01, etc.? Often this can be a slip in adding up or subtracting. (d) Does the error divide by 9? If it does it may be because someone has written 27 for 72, 36 for 63, 48 for 84 etc. In these cases, the error (45, 27, 36, etc.) always divides by 9. So if an error divides by 9 look for transposed figures. Some people are very prone to make this mistake. (e) Take one side of the trial balance from the other. Does anyone remember an entry for that amount – say £50.40? Someone might just remember it. (f) If this does not appear to be the case, divide the figure by 2 = £25.20. Have we got £25.20 on the wrong side? It would give us an error of twice the amount. (g) If none of these ideas helps, we must go right through the month's work checking every entry.

9 Suppose a trial balance comes out correctly, what can we now do?

(a) Congratulate ourselves on a month's work well done. (b) Go on and do final accounts if we want to.

Written Exercise: *Find out what is wrong with this trial balance.*

Account	Dr	Cr
Cash in hand	110.50	
Cash at bank	2 730.25	
Bank deposit		7 000.00
Premises	29 500.00	
Furniture	1 815.60	
Rent received	201.50	
Telephone	752.50	
Light and heat	386.00	
Purchases		24 248.00
Sales	36 500.00	
Bad debts	315.00	
Drawings	2 600.00	
Debtors	115.15	
Rent received		285.50
Capital		32 586.00
	£75 046.50	64 119.50

Go over the topic again until you are sure of all the answers. Then tick it off on the check list at the back of the book.

12 More about the trial balance

1 Which stock figure appears on the trial balance?

The opening stock – not the closing stock.

2 Why doesn't the closing stock appear?

Because we don't do the stocktaking until we have closed the books for the year and taken out the trial balance of the books.

3 At what stage does the closing stock come onto the books?

When we prepare the trading account. We clear the opening stock into the trading account and then bring on the closing stock, which also affects the trading account.

4 Suppose we do a trial balance and it balances. Are the books correct?

So far as we can tell at a first glance they are. We say a trial balance is *prima facie* (at a first sight) proof of the accuracy of the bookkeeping.

5 What mistakes might still exist?

There are five possible errors which do not show up on the trial balance. They are original errors, errors of omission, errors of commission, compensating errors and errors of principle.

6 What is an original error?

An error in the original documents that gave rise to an entry in the first place. If a supplier sent us an invoice for £100 instead of £1000 and we put it through our books we shall have a trial balance that agrees but when the error is discovered we must correct it.

7 What is an error of omission?

Where we leave a document out altogether. Suppose a credit note falls down the back of a radiator. We don't put it through our books – the trial balance agrees but the credit note has not been recorded.

8 What is an error of commission?

'Commission' means doing something. An error of commission means we do something wrong. For example, if we debit T. Hall with £50 which should have gone in P. Hall's account the trial balance will agree but both these accounts will be wrong.

9 What are compensating errors?

Errors which are equal in size but occur on opposite sides of the trial balance. A bookkeeper who is weak at addition or subtraction may make a £10 error in one account and a £10 error in another account. If these accounts come on opposite sides of the trial balance they will compensate for one another. The trial balance will agree, but it will be wrong in two places.

10 What are errors of principle?	These are errors caused by a failure to understand the principles of bookkeeping. For example if I buy goods for resale that is purchases, but if I buy furniture that is a capital item, the purchase of an asset. If an invoice for furniture is put through the purchases book and finishes up on the purchases account it will overstate the purchases and understate the furniture account.
11 In these special cases a trial balance does agree so we are not worried about the errors. When shall we start to worry about them?	When someone writes in and complains. For example, in (8) above T. Hall has been made a debtor for £50, and when we send him a statement he will complain.
12 Suppose a trial balance does not agree and we cannot find the error?	We open up a suspense account, which puts the trial balance right – because we make the entry on the side that is smaller. We now wait until something turns up to let us know the error – someone will complain sooner or later.
13 How do we correct errors?	With a journal entry (see Topic 13).

Written Exercise: *Tom Smith has a motor lorry surplus to requirements and valued on his books at £650. B. Prentice buys it from him, and receives an invoice payable at the end of the month. However, the bookkeeper enters the sale in the sales daybook. What sort of error is this? How shall we put it right?*

Go over the topic again until you are sure of all the answers. Then tick it off on the check list at the back of the book.

13 The correction of errors

1 What is difficult about correcting errors in bookkeeping?	Every error is different. We have to make up our minds what is wrong with the accounts and make entries to correct the error.

2 What is the general effect of errors?

Some account will be debited wrongly or some account will be credited wrongly. We have to restore the accounts to their correct position.

3 An invoice (£50) for the sale of goods to Mrs P Hall is debited by mistake to T Hall's account. How shall we correct the error?

We have to credit T Hall (to clear the debit entry made earlier) and debit Mrs P Hall to make her a debtor. Here is the journal entry:

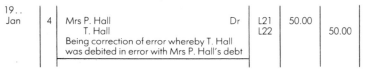

| 19.. Jan | 4 | Mrs P. Hall   Dr
 T. Hall
 Being correction of error whereby T. Hall <br> was debited in error with Mrs P. Hall's debt | L21
 L22 | 50.00 | 50.00 |

Fig. 13.1 A journal entry

4 A typewriter purchased from R Jones for £500 + VAT £50 has been entered in the Purchases daybook as purchases and posted to the ledger accounts. What kind of error is this?

It is an error of principle.

5 How shall we correct it?

The entry in Jones's account is correct, and we need not bother with it. The error is that instead of having £500 debited to the typewriters account it is muddled in with ordinary purchases in the purchases account. We must debit typewriters account and credit purchases account.

6 Make the journal entry for this

Here it is:

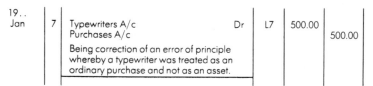

| 19.. Jan | 7 | Typewriters A/c   Dr
 Purchases A/c

 Being correction of an error of principle <br> whereby a typewriter was treated as an <br> ordinary purchase and not as an asset. | L7 | 500.00 | 500.00 |

Fig. 13.2 A journal entry

7 On paying R Smith you deducted 5 per cent cash discount (£38) but Smith has written to say the account was overdue and this discount cannot be allowed. How will you correct this?

The £38 should still be on the credit side of R Smith's account – we owe him the money. Instead it is on the credit side of discount received account as a profit. We must debit discount received account and credit R Smith. Then we had better pay him the money.

8 In putting through an entry for depreciation on the motor vehicles account the entry was correctly made in the depreciation account but credited to furniture and fittings account by mistake. How shall we correct this?

We must debit the furniture and fittings account to restore it to its correct position and credit motor vehicles account, to reduce the book value of the motor vehicles.

9 What is a one-sided journal entry?

A journal entry which is needed when an error only affects one side of the ledger.

10 Give an example

A Jones is debited with £279.50 for goods supplied to him, but the entry in Sales account is £297.50. The bookkeeper has crossed over two figures – sales account is £18.00 too large (on the credit side).

11 Make the journal entry

Here it is:

19.. Jan	15	Sales A/c Dr Being single-sided Journal entry caused by incorrect entry–figures transposed.	18.00	

Fig. 13.3 A journal entry

12 What error is sometimes made when posting the totals of the discount columns from the cash book to the ledger?

These are the only entries that don't change sides. The total of the discount allowed (on the debit side of the cash book) is posted to the debit side of discount allowed account. It is a very common error for someone to post it over to the opposite side – and credit the discount allowed account.

13 How shall we correct it? Suppose the total is £42.50.

It is on the credit side, and it should be on the debit side. To get it correct we have to debit the discount allowed account with twice the amount, i.e. with £85 in this case. This will be a single-sided journal entry.

14 A surplus motor vehicle valued on the books at £650 is cleared to a dealer for £400. The bookkeeper debits the cheque in the bank account and posts it to the credit side of motor vehicles account. What is wrong with this?

The rule is 'Remove the book value of the asset being sold from the books'. We should have credited motor vehicles with £650. £400 credited on the motor vehicles account means £250 still has to be accounted for. It is a loss – debit it in 'loss on sale of vehicle account', and credit it in the motor vehicles account to remove the rest of the book value.

15 When a trial balance will not agree, what do we do?

Open up a suspense account, with a balance on the necessary side (i.e. if we have a difference on the trial balance of £50 – the credit side being larger – we have to put the £50 on the debit side of suspense account to make the trial balance balance.

16 When we correct an error now, where will the double entry be for any error?

In the suspense account – so that eventually we clear it off as we discover the various errors causing it.

Written Exercise: *A suspense account has been opened with a debit balance of £524.00. Later A Smith writes to say that he has not been sent a statement for a machine supplied several weeks ago. We have forgotten to debit this in Smith's account. Make the journal entry.*

Go over the topic again until you are sure of all the answers. Then tick it off on the check list at the back of the book.

14 Stock records

1 How do we control stock?

With stock record cards of various sorts, bin cards, rack cards, tray cards, stock ledger cards.

2 What is the basic idea?

We keep a running balance on the card to show the current stock. Any stock that arrives is added and any stock that is requisitioned is deducted.

3 What document would accompany incoming stock?

An advice note, telling us what goods were being delivered. These would be entered in a 'Receipts (IN)' column and added to the balance in hand.

4 What would we do with the advice note?

Use it to prepare a goods received note, which is sent to accounts department. Then we would file it for future reference.

5 What document is used when stock is issued?

A requisition. The department that requires a particular part or unit raises a requisition, signed by a responsible person. This is used to authorise the issue of stock.

6 How would we enter the requisition?

It is entered in the 'Issued (OUT)' column, and deducted from the balance in hand.

Bin Card						
Description Bracket Max. Stock 100 Min. Stock 20 Re-order level 40				Bin number 1302 Part number A156 Re-order qty 50 Unit of issue 10		
Received			Issued			Balance
Date	Ref	Qty	Date	Ref	Qty	Qty
19..			19..			60
			17/4	R103	10	50
			29/4	R159	10	40
			5/5	R172	10	30
17/5	GRN 72	50				80

Fig. 14.1 A bin card

7 Consider the bin card in Fig. 14.1. What happened on 29 April and 17 May?

10 brackets were issued on 29 April.
50 brackets were received on 17 May.

8 What happens to the requisition after we have received it?

It is passed to costing department, where it will be priced and allocated to the job-cost sheet.

Written Exercise: *Draw up a record card for headed notepaper such as might be kept in the stationery store. Invent sensible stock figures, etc., and show 3 requisitions and 2 supplies of stock from the supplier. The firm employs 80 secretaries.*

Go over the topic again until you are sure of all the answers. Then tick it off on the check list at the back of the book.

15 Stock and the trading account

1 What is opening stock?

It is the stock we have in hand at the start of the financial year. It is what the old year hands on to the new year to be disposed of in the first few months of the new year.

2 Where does opening stock appear in the bookkeeping?

It stays on the stock account from the first day of the year until the last day of the year. Then it is cleared into the trading account as the first line on the debit side of the trading account.

3 Where does the opening stock figure come from?

It is the same as the closing stock at the end of the previous year. We find it by doing the stocktaking.

4 Our financial year ends on 31 December. What might we do in the last week of December?

Hold a stocktaking sale. We sell off as much stock as possible, clearing slow-moving items, so that there is less to count at stocktaking time.

5 When do we actually do the stocktaking?	Ideally – after close of work on 31 December. If we do it any other time we shall have to juggle with the figures. See Question 11 below.
6 How do we do the stocktaking?	(a) Count the stock, using a list of items in stock and physically checking how many of each type of item are present. (b) Value each item at cost price (or current selling price if lower. This would mean that the goods had deteriorated in some way). (c) Multiply the cost by the number of items to give the value of each set. (d) Add these together to get the total stock value.
7 What happens to this closing stock value?	It will be used in the trading account, and will eventually become the opening stock figure for next year.
8 Explain the entries made in the stock account at the end of the year	(a) First we transfer the opening stock figure, which is on the debit side of stock account, to the trading account. The journal entry is: Debit trading account and credit stock account. The stock account is now clear. (b) We now take on the closing stock, which has to be credited in the trading account and debited in the stock account. It thus becomes the opening stock for next year and stays on the debit side of stock account for a whole year. The three stages of the stock account are shown in Fig. 15.1 overleaf.
9 Now explain the same entries for the trading account – putting in any other entries that help your explanation	(a) Transferring the opening stock brings it in on the debit side of the trading account. (b) Transferring the closing stock should bring it in on the credit side of the trading account – but remember

that to keep the account in good style we don't put it on the credit side. We *deduct it* from the debit side. This brings out the 'cost of stock sold'. This is shown in Fig. 15.2.

10 Suppose we can't do the stocktaking on the last day of the financial year?

We do it when it is convenient – as close as possible to the last day – and we have to adjust the figures for stock coming in and out in the few days between.

(i)

	Stock Account				L1
19.. Jan 1	Balance	£ 3250			

(ii)

	Stock Account				L1
19.. Jan 1	Balance	£ 3250	19.. Dec 31	Trading A/c	£ 3250

(iii)

	Stock Account				L1
19.. Jan 1	Balance	£ 3250	19.. Dec 31	Trading A/c	£ 3250
19.. Jan 1	Balance	£ 4725			

Fig. 15.1 Stock accounts

	Trading Account				L102
19.. Dec 31	Op. stock Purchases	£ 3 250 27 500	19.. Dec 31	Sales	£ 46 750
	Total stock available *Less* closing stock	30 750 4 725			
	Cost of stock sold Gross profit	26 025 20 725			
		£46 750			£46 750

Fig. 15.2 Trading account

11 Suppose we do it on 29 December and it comes to £3820. What adjustments would we need to make?	(a) We make the stock in hand £3820 on 29 December. (b) If any stock comes in on 30 and 31 December we must add it on at cost price. (c) If any stock is sold we must deduct it (at cost price) because it won't be in stock on 31 December.
12 Suppose we took stock on 2 January and want to know what the stock was on 31 December	We must work it out the opposite way: (a) Deduct any stock that came in on 1 and 2 January. (b) Add on, at cost price, any stock sold on 1 and 2 January – because it was still in stock on 31 December.

Written Exercise: *M Drucker finds stock is £3850 on 27 March – his financial year ends on 31 March.*

During the last four days of March stock worth £386 is delivered, and sales total £870, of which 33⅓ per cent is profit. Sales returned to him totalled £15 at selling price, but 33⅓ per cent of that was profit. What was the correct stock figure at 31 March?

Go over the topic again until you are sure of all the answers. Then tick it off on the check list at the back of the book.

16 Bank reconciliation statements

1 What is a bank reconciliation statement?	A statement which brings together the bank account figures in the cash book and the figures in the bank account at the bank, and proves that even though they are different, they are really both correct.
2 Why should these figures differ?	For a number of reasons, connected with time-lags, and the way in which entries are made.

3 Give examples

(a) Each party (our own accounts department and the bank itself) does not know immediately what the other is doing. For example, the bank may charge us interest, but we shall not find out until we ask for a statement. We may write a cheque but they won't know about it until it is presented. (b) There are always time-lags. If we send a cheque to A.B. to settle a debt, we shall enter it in our cash book today. A.B. may not get it until tomorrow, and may not pay it in for several days. Then it has to go through the clearing service. (c) Either side may make an error that the other side will know nothing about.

4 Suppose we get a bank statement. What do we do with it when it arrives?

(a) Compare the items on it with the items on our cash book and tick all those items that appear in both records. (b) Now we look at the other items. Which of them are items we did not know about until now? They could be: (i) interest or other charges taken by the bank; (ii) direct debits taken by the bank; (iii) credit transfers received from someone on our behalf, wages, dividends on gilt-edged securities, etc. All these items must now be entered in our cash book to bring it up to date. This will alter our balance in the cash book and bring it closer to the bank's statement. (c) Now we look at the items in our cash book that don't yet appear in the bank statement. These will be cheques paid in but not yet cleared, and cheques paid out but not yet presented to the bank for payment. It is these items that will have to appear on the bank reconciliation statement. (d) If we find any errors we must put them right – for example, we may have entered a cheque for £19.75 as £19.57. We must correct this by entering another 18 pence.

5 Here is a bank reconciliation statement. Explain it

Bank Reconciliation Statement
as at 4 April 19 . .

	£
Balance per cash book	1 275.63
less Cheques paid in	
but not yet cleared	
T Smith 168.50	
R Jones 37.75	
	206.25
	1 069.38
add back Cheques drawn but	
not yet presented at	
bank by recipients	
M Law 138.25	
A Castle 26.50	
	164.75
Balance as per	
bank statement	£1 234.13

It starts with the balance on the cash book, and works towards the bank statement. The cheques paid in but not yet cleared are entered in our cash book but the bank has not yet given us the money. So we must deduct them, as the bank statement does not know about them. The cheques drawn, but not yet presented to the bank for payment have been deducted from our cash book but the bank is not yet aware of these cheques. So we must add them back again. We have now reconciled the cash book with the bank statement.

6 Which book is a bank reconciliation statement entered in?

None at all – it is done on a piece of paper.

7 What do we do with it?

We type it out neatly and file it away for reference purposes.

8 When will we need to refer to it?

Next month.

9 Why?

Because each month the first thing to do is to make sure that all the outstanding cheques from the previous bank reconciliation statement have in fact now been cleared. If they have, we can go on and reconcile this month's items.

Written Exercise: *On 31 July M Lawrence's cash book shows a balance at the bank of £425.15. On asking the bank for a statement, he finds it shows that he has £298.94. On checking, he sees the following differences: the bank has paid a mortgage instalment of £95.70 on a standing order, and it has also debited him with £12.76 bank charges. Two cheques sent to R Marsden (£17.50) and B Dark (£37.25) have not yet been presented, and a cheque for £72.50 that he paid in from R Guy has not yet been cleared.*
You are asked (a) to put the cash book right where it is wrong; and (b) to make out a bank reconciliation statement for the remaining items.

Go over the topic again until you are sure of all the answers. Then tick it off on the check list at the back of the book.

17 Capital and revenue expenditure

1 What is capital expenditure?

Expenditure on assets which are purchased for long-term use in the business and are not to be resold except at the end of their life.

2 Name five capital assets

(a) Land and buildings. (b) Plant and machinery. (c) Furniture and fittings. (d) Motor vehicles. (e) Typewriters.

3 What are the ledger entries when we purchase assets?

(a) Always debit the asset account. (b) Credit one of the following: (i) cash account if we pay cash; (ii) bank account if we pay by cheque; (iii) the creditor, if we obtain the assets on credit.

4 What is revenue expenditure?

Expenditure on items that only last the business a relatively short time, and are then used up completely.

5 Give examples

(a) Postage stamps. (b) Light and heat. (c) Telephone expenses. (d) Wages. (e) Carriage in. (f) Carriage out.

6 What are the ledger entries for revenue expenditure?

(a) Debit the expense account – it becomes one of the losses of the business. (b) Credit (i) cash account if we pay cash; (ii) bank account, if we pay by cheque; (iii) the creditor, if the item was supplied on credit.

7 What is the boundary line in time between capital and revenue expenditure?

One year. Generally speaking, if an item lasts longer than one year it is an asset, if it lasts less than one year it is a revenue expense.

8 There are a few areas which might be called 'grey' areas, where we are not quite sure whether things are capital expenditure or revenue expenditure. What are they?

(a) Things like redecorations. They are rather temporary, but may only be done every three years. (b) Some revenue expenses result in the creation of capital items. These should be capitalised – as where our workers build an extension to the canteen.

9 What do we do with things like redecorations?

(a) Capitalise the revenue expense – put it in an account such as the decorations in suspense account. (b) Write off one-third of this each year in the profit and loss account, so that each year carries a fair share of the cost.

10 What do we do about activities that increase the value of assets?

Capitalise the revenue expense. Suppose we buy a machine for £20 000 and our own maintenance people build concrete platforms, supply electricity, etc., at a cost of £1000 for materials and £4000 for wages. We take the machine on the books at £25 000 (debit machinery account) and credit the supplier £20 000, wages account £4000 and purchases account £1000 (for the materials used).

11 Why is it important to distinguish between capital and revenue expenditure (and also capital and revenue receipts)?

Because it is a rule in bookkeeping that we must each year: (a) work out our profits correctly so that we pay the correct amount of tax; (b) produce a correct balance sheet, which gives a true and fair view of the business, its assets and liabilities.

12 Where do the revenue items come into this picture?

When we work out our profits – it is the revenue items that come in the trading account and the profit and loss account.

13 And where do the capital items come into the picture?

They produce the balance sheet.

Written Exercise: *In the business of a cafe proprietor, which of the following would be capital expenditure and which revenue expenditure: (a) purchase of meat, salad, etc. for lunches: (b) purchase of a bread-slicing machine; (c) wages of staff; (d) gas and electricity bills; (e) purchase of cutlery? The proprietor decides to extend the cafe into the backyard, with the help of two of his employees. It costs £850 for materials, £600 in wages and the increased value is agreed to be £3000 on the property. How would you enter these matters in the books if the increase in value over the cost is deemed to be a capital profit not a revenue profit?*

Go over the topic again until you are sure of all the answers. Then tick it off on the check list at the back of the book.

18 Final accounts – 1: the trial balance

1 Where do final accounts start?

With the trial balance at the end of the last month of the financial year.

2 What is the title of the trial balance?

Trial balance as at (date) 19... It always gives the date the trial balance was extracted from the ledger

3 What sort of items do we have on the debit side of a trial balance?

There will be debit balances on the following: (a) All the asset accounts; premises account, machinery account etc. These are the *real accounts*. (b) All the loss accounts – the *nominal accounts which are losses*. For example, rent and rates, light and heat, motor vehicle expenses. (c) The drawings account. This is what the owner of the business has drawn out in expectation of profits.

4 Some of the 'loss' accounts are trading account items. They will be used to find the gross profit in the trading account. Which are they?

The purchases account, the sales returns account and the stock (which has the opening stock on it from the start of the financial year). There may also be some expenses directly concerned with trading activities which ought to be deducted from the profits in the trading account (such as warehouse wages, carriage in, etc.)

5 Which sort of accounts do we have on the credit side of the trial balance?

(a) All the liabilities – loans, mortgages, debentures (for companies) and the bank overdraft, if there is one. (b) All the 'profit' accounts, the *nominal accounts that are profits*. These include sales, commission received, discount received, etc. (c) The capital account – a special kind of liability – the liability to the owner of the business.

6 Some of these credit items will also be used in the trading account. Which ones?

The sales account and the purchases returns account.

7 There is one other figure we need before we can do the final accounts. It is not in the trial balance. Which is it?

It is the closing stock figure. We must do the stocktaking.

8 Are there any tricky items in the trial balance?

Yes. (a) *Returns in and returns out.* Returns in are sales returns, and appear on the debit side (we receive the goods back). Returns out are purchases returns and are on the credit side (We give the goods back). (b) *Carriage in and carriage out*. These are both losses and appear on the debit side. The reason we split the carriage in this way is because carriage in goes in the trading account and carriage out in the profit and loss account. (c) *Provisions for bad debts and provisions for depreciation*. These are not loss accounts. They appear on the credit side – they are profits tucked away to provide for these losses should they occur.

Written Exercise: *Draw up a trial balance from these figures, extracted from the books of L Tasker at 31 December 19. .*

Warehouse wages	*720.50*
Sales	*32 600.00*
Purchases	*21 040.00*
Cash in hand	*280.65*
Freehold property	*12 600.00*
Sundry debtors	*650.50*
Stock in trade at start	*1 530.75*
Sundry creditors	*600.95*
Bank overdraft	*2 000.00*
Plant and machinery	*8 000.00*
Returns inward	*200.05*
Discount received	*201.50*
Capital	*7 620.00*
Rent and rates	*1 220.00*
Office expenses	*1 780.00*
Loan from A. Bank Ltd	*5 000.00*

Go over the topic again until you are sure of all the answers. Then tick it off on the check list at the back of the book.

19 Final accounts— 2: the trading account

1 What is the trading account?

It is the account where we work out the gross profit on trading.

2 How is the account headed?

Trading Account for year ended 31 December 19... Of course it could be done quarterly or monthly, but the point is it works out the profits in a stated period.

3 What is the simplest way of looking at gross profit?

It is the difference between what we buy things for and what we sell them for. So in the simplest form:

Trading Account for year ended 31 December 19...

Purchases	8 000	Sales	20 000
Gross profit	12 000		
	£20 000		£20 000

4 This is too simple. How must we adjust it?

Some of the purchases and some of the sales are returned. So a better figure would be:

Trading Account for year ended 31 December 19...

Purchases	8 000	Sales	20 000
less Returns	300	*less* Returns	1 500
Net purchases	7 700	Net sales	18 500
Gross profit	10 800	(Net turnover)	
	£18 500		£18 500

5 Why is 'net turnover' an important term?

It is used to describe the actual sales of a business (i.e. sales less returns) and is the term most widely used when selling a business, or taking over a company. The buyer wants to know what the 'turnover' of the business is.

6 What aspect of trading has still not been taken into account in the trading account in 4 above?

The stock positions. Except in its first year of business every trading enterprise has 'opening stock' at the start of the year, and 'closing stock' at the end of the year.

7 Where do these stock figures come into the trading account?

For convenience we arrange to have them dealt with on the debit side as an adjustment to the purchases figure. The point is that we don't actually sell exactly what we purchase. The purchases have to be added to the opening stock to give the 'total stock available', and the closing stock – which has not been sold – is taken away from this figure, to give the cost of stock sold.

8 Show this debit side of the trading account with some imaginary figures

		£
Opening stock		3 200
add **Purchases**	8000	
less **Returns**	300	
		7 700
Total stock available		10 900
less **Closing stock**		2 850
Cost of stock sold		8 050
Gross profit (using £18 500 – the net sales figure in 4 above)		
		10 450
		£18 500

9 Is that quite all we need to do on the trading account?

No, there are one or two special matters we must also attend to if they come up in our businesses (or in examination questions).

10 What are they?

They concern certain expenses which are incurred as part of the process of obtaining goods for sale, rather than as general overheads. These expenses are really trading expenses, and should be included in the trading account rather than in the profit and loss account. The most important are: (a) carriage in; (b) Customs duty on imported purchases. These are really increases in the cost of purchases and should be added to purchases in the trading account.

Another group are expenses incurred in storing goods before sale – such as warehouse wages and warehouse expenses. These should be added to the 'cost of stock sold' to give a final figure – cost of sales. When the cost of sales is deducted from the net turnover we get the gross profit.

11 Illustrate these improvements in the style of the trading account

This is given in Fig. 19.1.

Trading Account
For year ended 31 December 19. .

Dec 31		£	Dec 31	£
Opening stock		3 200	Sales	20 000
Purchases	8 000		*less* Returns	1 500
add Carriage in	650		Net turnover	18 500
add Customs duty	425			
	9 075			
less Returns	300			
Net purchases		8 775		
Total stock available		11 975		
less Closing stock		2 850		
Cost of stock sold		9 125		
Warehouse wages		2 150		
Warehouse expenses		875		
Cost of sales		12 150		
Gross profit		6 350		
		£18 500		£18 500

Fig. 19.1

12 In presenting a trading account in this advanced style we have adapted double-entry in three places. What are they?

At three points, instead of putting things on their correct side, we have deducted them from the other side. This has the same result, but it gives a much better display of important figures.

13 Explain these cases

(a) We have not put purchases returns on the credit side – we have deducted them from the debit side to give the net purchases figure. (b) Similarly we have not put sales returns on the debit side, we have deducted them from the credit side to give us the net sales (net turnover) figure. (c) We have not put closing stock on the credit side – we have deducted it from the debit side to bring out the 'cost of stock sold'.

14 To get good marks in an examination, what sort of trading account must you produce?

One in good style, like Fig. 19.1 (though an examination exercise would rarely have all the expenses shown – perhaps only 'carriage in' would appear).

Written Exercise: *Prepare a trading account for the year ended 31 December 19. . for P Marshall from the following information: Opening stock £1756.50; Purchases £37 250; Carriage in £495.50; Customs duty on imported purchases £1528.50; Purchases returns £874.00; Closing stock £3556.50; Wages of warehouse workers £7650.00; Warehouse expenses £2120.00; Sales £85 550.00; Sales returns £1550.00.*

Go over the topic again until you are sure of all the answers. Then tick it off on the check list at the back of the book.

20 Final accounts– 3: the profit and loss

1 What is the profit and loss account?

It is that part of the final accounts where we work out the net profit of the business.

2 What does 'net' profit mean?

It means 'clean' profit – from the French word 'nettoyer' to clean.

3 What does the profit and loss account start with?

The gross profit brought down from the trading account, on the credit side. (Of course in very rare cases it could start with a gross loss brought down on the debit side from the trading account.)

4 Why does it turn the gross profit into a net profit?

Because in the profit and loss account we deduct all the expenses of the business, rent, rates, light, heat, telephone expenses, etc., from the gross profit to leave the clean (or pure) profit which is the final result of the business's activities.

5 Is there anything else in the profit and loss account besides the gross profit and the deductions from it (the expenses of the business)?

Yes. There are a few other sources of profit that have to be added to the gross profit before we deduct the expenses.

6 Give some examples

The commonest are rent received, discount received and commission received. We might also have a profit on the sale of assets. This has to be taken in on the profit and loss account because it means that excessive depreciation was deducted in earlier years – so the profit on the sale must be treated as a revenue receipt (not a capital receipt).

7 Make up an imaginary profit and loss account including typical items

Profit and Loss Account
for year ending 31 December 19. .

19. .	£	19. .	£
Rent	2435	Gross profit	18785
Rates	843	Discount received	385
Salaries	6525	Rent received	624
Telephone expenses	824		19794
Office expenses	368		
Fares, etc.	124		
Motor expenses	1568		
	12687		
Net profit	7107		
	£19794		£19794
		Net profit	7107

8 Why is the net profit brought down in the profit and loss account?

It would be absolutely wrong not to bring it down, since it would appear that the account was clear. It is not clear. We have to give the profit to whoever is entitled to it.

9 Who is entitled to the profits of a business?

The proprietor(s). The sole trader, or the partners, or the shareholders of the company – provided the directors recommend a dividend.

10 What actually happens to the net profit?

In the case of sole traders it is carried to the credit side of capital account. In the case of partnerships and companies it is carried to the credit side of the appropriation account, where it can be given to the appropriate people – the partners or the shareholders.

11 In (7) above the profit and loss account resulted in a profit. What would it have looked like if the result had been a loss?

The right-hand side (the profits) would have been smaller than the left-hand side (the losses) and the net loss would have come in on the right-hand side and been carried down to the left-hand side as net loss £. . . .

12 When this was transferred to a sole trader's capital account what would it have done?

It would have reduced his capital, as shown below:

Capital Account (A. Grocer)

19..	£	19..	£
Dec 31 Net loss	4 250	Jan 1 Balance	13 550
31 Drawings in year	3 500		
31 Balance	5 800		
	£13 550		£13 550
		19. 1	
		Jan 1 Balance	5 800

13 What can we say of A Grocer?

In 19.. he was living off his capital.

14 Not all businesses have a trading account and a profit and loss account. Why not?

Because not all businesses trade. If a business supplies a service there is no trading, only a profit and loss account is needed. The fees received are the chief profits, and the expenses are set against them. Some professional people dislike the words profit and loss account – a doctor does not like to think he is making profit out of Mrs Jones's illness.

15 What do professional people call the profit and loss account?

The income and expenditure account.

Written Exercise: *From the following particulars prepare the trading account and then the profit and loss account of M Morgan, for the year ending 31 December 19...*

	£
Stock at start, Jan 1 19. .	*2034*
Discount received	*137*
Insurance premiums	*405*
Salaries	*2500*
Purchases	*28 250*
Returns outward	*240*
Printing and stationery	*856*
Rent and rates	*1000*
Sales	*44 160*
Returns inwards	*350*
General expenses	*1245*
Telephone account	*660*
Stock 31 DEc 19. .	*3250*
Discount allowed	*540*
Interest paid on loans	*185*
Light and heat	*265*

Go over the topic again until you are sure of all the answers. Then tick it off on the check list at the back of the book.

21 Final accounts – 4: the balance sheet

1 What is a balance sheet?

It is a snapshot of the affairs of a business taken at a moment in time – usually after work has finished on the last day of the financial year (but you can take out a balance sheet at any time).

2 What does it consist of?

It is ia list of the assets and liabilities on the books of the business after the trading and profit and loss accounts have been prepared.

3 What does the preparation of these accounts do to the trial balance of the books?

It clears all the loss accounts and all the profit accounts so that they no longer have balances on them, and therefore disappear from the trial balances, leaving only the assets and liabilities on the trial balance. One or two special cases are worth noting.

4 What are these?

(a) The **stock account**, which used to show the opening stock, now shows the closing stock. (b) The **profit and loss account** now has a balance on it – usually the net profit, but it could be a net loss. (c) The **drawing account** is still open – we shall deal with it when we do the balance sheet.

5 How is the balance sheet headed?

Balance Sheet, as at 31 December, 19.., or whatever the date might be.

6 What is the best way to do a balance sheet?

Strictly speaking, the assets should be on the left and the liabilities on the right. Because of a mistake made in an Act of Parliament in 1856, British balance sheets are often done the wrong way round – liabilities on the left and assets on the right. It is best to stick to the way you have learned at college/school. In this revision book we have done them both ways to show both methods.

7 What is a vertical balance sheet?

It is a way of doing a balance sheet which helps the presentation of advanced accounts. It is dealt with in *Bookkeeping and Accounts – 2*, but don't worry about it at present.

8 What are the two ways of displaying a balance sheet?

The **order of permanence** and the **order of liquidity.**

9 What is the difference?

With the order of permanence we put the most permanent items first, fixed assets before current assets.
With the order of liquidity we put the least permanent items first, current assets before fixed assets.

10 Who uses which method?

Most manufacturing and trading firms use the order of permanence. Banks usually use the order of liquidity.

11 What sort of balance sheet is this?

It is a traditional British balance sheet in the order of permanence.

Balance Sheet
as at 31 December 19. .

	£	£			£	£
Capital			*Fixed assets*			
At start		30 109	Land and buildings			38 500
add: Profits	11 200		Machinery			27 250
less: Drawings	4 250		Furniture			4 850
		6 950	Motor vehicles			7 255
		37 059				77 855
Long-term liabilities			*Current assets*			
Mortgage	30 000		Closing stock	4 254		
Bank loan	15 000		Debtors	1 875		
		45 000	Cash at bank	2 309		
			Cash in hand	184		
					8 622	
Current liabilities						
Creditors	3 785					
Rates due	478					
Wages due	155					
		4 418				
Fig. 21.1		£86 477				£86 477

12 Supposing it was in the order of liquidity, what would be the difference?	The current liabilities and the current assets would be at the top, and the whole order would be reversed (i.e. cash in hand would be the first asset and not the last).
13 What kind of a balance sheet is this?	It is a non-traditional balance sheet in correct style (assets on the left, liabilities on the right) and it is also in the order of liquidity (not permanence).

Balance Sheet
as at 31 December 19. .

Current assets		£	Current liabilities		£
Cash in hand		184	Wages due		155
Cash at bank		2 309	Rates due		478
Debtors		1 875	Creditors		3 785
Closing stock		4 254			4 418
		8 622			
Fixed assets			Long-term liabilities		
Motor vehicles	7 255		Bank loan	15 000	
Furniture	4 850		Mortgage	30 000	
Machinery	27 250				45 000
Land and buildings	38 500				
		77 855			
			Capital		
			at start		30 109
			add: Profits	11 200	
			less: Drawings	4 250	
				6 950	
					37 059
		£86 477			£86 477

Fig. 21.2

Written Exercise: *Here is the trial balance of M Williams at 31 March, 19...*
You are to prepare his trading, and profit and loss accounts for the year ending 31 March, 19.., and his balance sheet as at that date.

	Dr	Cr
Office salaries	7 215.50	
Discount allowed and received	195.00	259.65
Rent	3 400.00	
Capital		40 000.00
Debtors and creditors	1 565.00	959.80
Cash	187.50	
Plant and machinery	14 800.00	
Stock at 1 April previous year	3 500.00	
Carriage inwards	300.00	
Carriage outwards	495.00	
Purchases and sales	27 565.00	62 756.50
Premises	30 000.00	
Cash at bank	10 361.45	
Drawings	4 500.00	
Returns – in and out	156.50	265.00
	£104 240.95	£104 240.95

Stock on 31 March, 19.., was valued at £1975.50.

Go over the topic again until you are sure of all the answers. Then tick it off on the check list at the back of the book.

22 Adjustments in final accounts

1 What are adjustments?

They are changes in the amount of any expenses of the business or receipts of the business to establish the true amounts paid or received in the financial year.

2 What is the principle behind them?

There are two principles really: (a) that each year should carry every penny of expense properly incurred in that year, but no more. It should also take account of every bit of income earned in that year, but no more. (b) that the balance sheet should present a 'true and fair view' of the affairs of the business at the end of the financial year.

3 Who imposed these requirements upon accounts?	They are traditional, since accountancy first began, but for companies they are actually enacted into law in the Companies Act 1985. However, the principles apply to all business.
4 What do these principles ensure?	That the final accounts (a) result in an accurate figure for profits for the year, so that the trader knows what his true income is (and so does the tax inspector); (b) that the balance sheet is honest and accurate (so far as it can be). Businesses are bought and sold on the basis of balance sheet valuations; so an accurate balance sheet enables business transfers to take place honestly and to the mutual benefit of both parties.

Special Note: Revise and Test Bookkeeping and Accounts 2

A full discussion of adjustments is included in Book 2, which you should use to continue your revision course in Bookkeeping and Accounts. Topics covered in Book 2 include:

Adjustments in final accounts; partnership accounts; limited liability companies' accounts; non-profit making organisations; manufacturing accounts; departmental accounts; control accounts; the purchase of businesses; amalgamations; accounting concepts; the interpretation of final accounts.